D0578417

Published by Smart Apple Media,
an imprint of Black Rabbit Books
P.O. Box 3263, Mankato, Minnesota 56002
www.blackrabbitbooks.com

Published by arrangement with
The Salariya Book Company Ltd

Cataloging-in-Publication Data is available
from the Library of Congress

Printed in the United States
At Corporate Graphics,
North Mankato, Minnesota

9 8 7 6 5 4 3 2 1

ISBN: 978-1-62588-351-3

contents

making a start

The key to drawing well is learning to look carefully. Study your subject till you know it really well. Keep a sketchbook with you and draw whenever you get the chance. Even doodling is good—it helps to make your drawing more confident. You'll soon develop your own style of drawing, but this book will help you to find your way.

Practice drawing stick figures for basic poses.

quick sketches

Try sketching details from books or magazines.

perspective

Perspective is a way of drawing objects so that they look as though they have three dimensions. Note how the part that is closest to you looks larger, and the part furthest away from you looks smaller. That's just how things look in real life.

The vanishing point (V.P.) is the place in a perspective drawing where parallel lines appear to meet. The position of the vanishing point depends on the viewer's eye level.

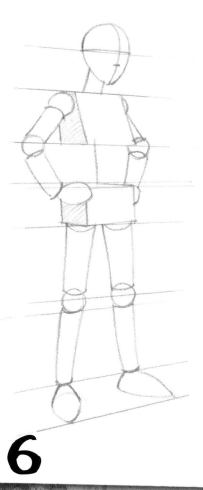

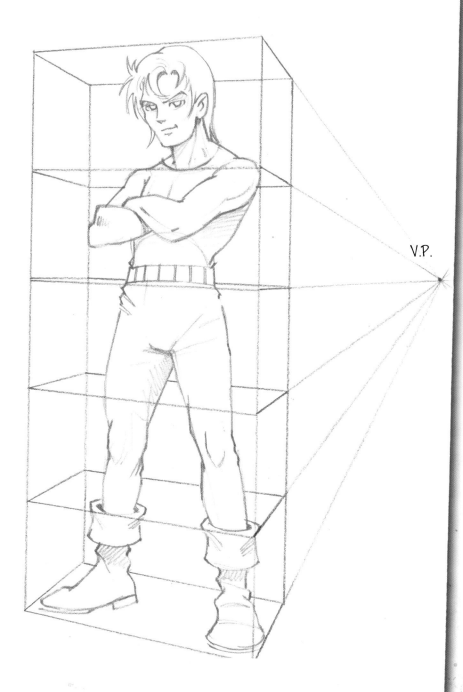

V.P.

two-point perspective drawing

Two-point perspective uses two vanishing points: one for lines running along the length of the subject, and one on the opposite side for lines running across the width of the subject.

In this drawing the vanishing points are very low. This gives the impression that you are looking up at the figure—very dramatic!

V.P.

V.P.

Low eye level
(view from below)

V.P.

V.P.

High eye level
(view from above)

Three-point perspective adds a third vanishing point above or below the drawing (above right.)

V.P. = vanishing point

V.P.

7

materials

Remember, the best equipment and materials will not necessarily make the best drawing—only practice will.

pencils

Try out different grades of pencils. Hard pencils make fine gray lines and soft pencils make softer, darker marks.

erasers

are useful for cleaning up drawings and removing construction lines.

paper

Bristol paper is good for crayons, pastels, and felt-tip pens. Watercolor paper is thicker; it is the best choice for water-based paints or inks.

Use this sandpaper block if you want to shape your pencil to a really sharp point.

inks

Use colored inks straight from the bottle or dilute them with water.

Ink

Mixing palette

felt-tip pens

Felt-tips usually come in sets of mixed colors. The ones that make very thin lines are called fineliners.

Fineliners

Dip-in pen nibs

Brushes

Correction fluid

Gouache

Watercolors

pens

Technical drawing pens have cartridges which can be refilled or replaced. Old-fashioned dip-in pens are much cheaper and come in many different styles and sizes.

paints

Ordinary watercolors are translucent (see-through); gouache is not. Try other kinds of paints, too.

Technical drawing pens

9

styles

Try different types of drawing papers and materials. Experiment with pens, from felt-tips to ballpoints, and make interesting marks. What happens if you draw with pen and ink on wet paper?

Felt-tips come in a range of line widths. The wider pens are good for filling in large areas of flat tone.

Ink silhouette

Silhouette is a style of drawing which mainly relies on solid dark shapes.

10

Pencil drawings can include a vast amount of detail and tone. Try different grades of pencil to get a range of light and shade effects in your drawings.

Lines drawn in **ink** cannot be erased, so unless you are very confident you may want to sketch your drawing in pencil first.

Hatching   Cross-hatching

It can be tricky adding light and shade to a drawing with a pen. Use a solid layer of ink for the very darkest areas and cross-hatching (straight lines criss-crossing each other) for ordinary dark tones. Use hatching (straight lines running parallel to each other) for midtones.

11

body proportions

Heads in manga are drawn slightly bigger than in real life. Legs and hips make up more than half the overall height of the figure.

Drawing a stick figure is the simplest way to make decisions about a pose. It helps you see how different positions can change the center of balance.

You often see heroes in dramatic poses. Experiment with poses like this.

Proportions of a hero:

The eye level is about midway down the head.

Shoulders

Hips

Knees

Feet

Standing straight

inking

Here's one way of inking over your final pencil drawing.

Refillable inking pens come in various tip sizes. The tip is what determines the width of the line that is drawn. Sizes include: 0.1, 0.5, 1.0, 2.0 mm.

Different tones of ink can be used to add depth to the drawing.
Mix ink with water to achieve the tones you need.

Correction fluid usually comes in small bottles or in pen format. This can be useful for cleaning up ink lines.

heads

Manga heads have a distinctive style and shape. Drawing different facial expressions is very important— it shows instantly what your character is thinking or feeling.

1. Start by drawing a square. Fit the head, chin, and neck inside it to keep the correct proportions. Draw two construction lines to position the top of the ear and the base of the nose.

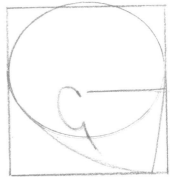

2. Add an oversized manga-style eye and draw the mouth and nose.

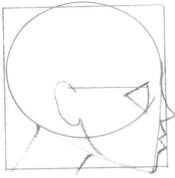

3. Add a pupil to the eye and draw an eyebrow.

4. Draw some manga-style hair.

1. Draw a circle. Add construction lines through its center point.

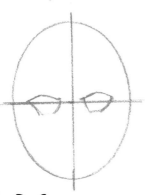

2. Using the construction lines, position the eyes, ears, and mouth.

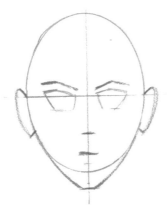

3. Then draw them in.

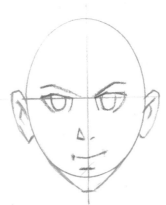

4. Draw the hair.

Practice drawing heads from different angles and with different facial expressions.

Center line

Whichever way the head is turned, the nose and mouth always stay on the center line.

Child

Female

Male

Male heads, by contrast, have thicker necks and a squared-off, chiseled jawline. They also have slightly smaller eyes than females and wider mouths.

15

creases and folds

C lothes fall into natural creases and folds when worn. Look at real people to see how fabric drapes and how it falls into creases. This will help you to dress your characters more realistically.

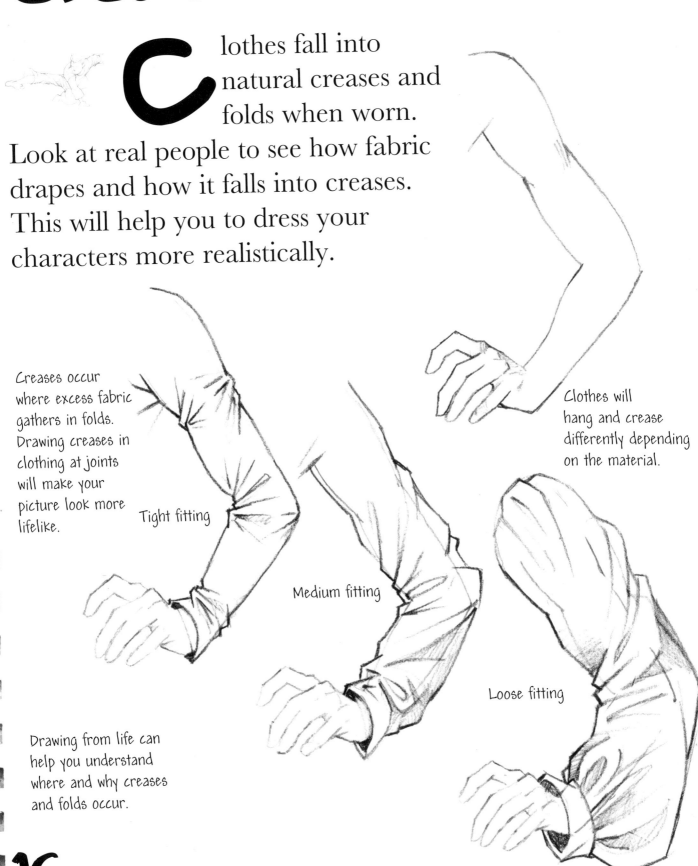

Creases occur where excess fabric gathers in folds. Drawing creases in clothing at joints will make your picture look more lifelike.

Tight fitting

Medium fitting

Loose fitting

Clothes will hang and crease differently depending on the material.

Drawing from life can help you understand where and why creases and folds occur.

16

The way fabric is drawn can instantly give a sense of movement and action to a pose.

Shading clothes is also very important. Think of all the places the light won't reach, such as inside trouser legs.

hiro

Hiro is the king of the warriors. He is young, reckless, and very brave. His samurai swords have magical powers, and were left to him by his ancient master.

1. Draw ovals for the head, body, and hips. Add center lines to divide the head vertically and horizontally. These will help you to place the ears and the nose.

Sketch an outline for Hiro's sword.

2. Add lines for the spine and the angle of the hips and shoulders.

Gradually build up long hair like this by adding wisps.

3. Draw stick arms and legs, with dots where the joints are. Add outline shapes for hands and feet.

4. Using the construction lines as a guide, start to build up the main shapes and features.

These little circles are to remind you where the elbows and knees go.

Sword in belt

5. Draw the clothes, hair, and facial features. This is where your drawing really starts to come to life.

Why not try finishing this drawing off in ink?

6. If you don't want your construction lines to show, erase them before you do the final shading and details.

7. Now finish all the little details of the clothes, hair, and face, and the shading. Don't rush! The more carefully you do these finishing touches, the better your drawing will look.

Hiro's clothes and armor are quite complex. Try looking at pictures of warriors to get a feel for the type of clothes they might wear.

19

space boy

Space boy flies in zero gravity toward us in his specially modified space suit with power gauntlets.

1. Draw a circle for the head and ovals for the body and hips.

2. Add lines for the spine and the angle of the hips and shoulders.

3. Draw stick arms and legs with dots for the joints and shapes for the hands and feet.

4. Use your guidelines to sketch in the neck, facial features, and hair.

Small circles indicate the positions of elbows and knees.

5. Using the construction lines as a guide, start drawing in the main shapes of the body.

Think about perspective here. Use front-end perspective to make the head and shoulders bigger and the legs and feet smaller—this way it looks like space boy is coming right at us!

20

Power gauntlets

6. Now start to sketch out the
final shapes of clothes, hair,
arms, and legs.

Lines across the
mask give it a
reflective look.

Think about little details
of space boy's power
gauntlets and boots.

Finished off
in ink

7. If you don't want your construction lines
to show, erase them carefully before you
add the finishing touches: shading, facial
features, patterns on the clothes.

the sorceress

The sorceress is very powerful and knows all the secrets of the earth. She keeps bad spirits away and can turn enemies to stone.

1. Draw ovals for the head and body.

2. Add lines for the spine and the angle of the shoulders.

3. Draw stick arms with dots for the joints and shapes for the hands.

4. Using your construction lines, sketch in the facial features and hair shape.

Try sketching from real life to get a feel for the positions of fingers.

Put it in perspective! This hand is closest to us, therefore it is much bigger.

5. Flesh out the arms, legs, and body, and add more detail to the face. Sketch the basic outline of the sorceress's wand.

6. Draw the shapes of the billowing hair and cloak. The facial expression should be dramatic but smiling.

7. Erase your construction lines if you don't want them to show.

8. Take plenty of time to finish the details of the face and hair, the cloak, and the wand.

Flyaway hair creates a dramatic effect and creates the impression of movement and wind.

Long, elegant fingers help to give her character.

Shading shows which way her cloak and hair are blowing.

Wood detail on the wand.

If you want a different final look to your drawing you can try finishing it in ink. Carefully go over any outlines, and then remove any leftover pencil lines with an eraser.

23

dragon girl

Dragon girl possesses magic cards which can unleash the power of various mighty dragons.

1. Draw different-sized ovals for the head, body, and hips. This time, add another oval for the dragon's head.

2. Add a line for the spine and others to show the angle of the hips and shoulders.

Magic card

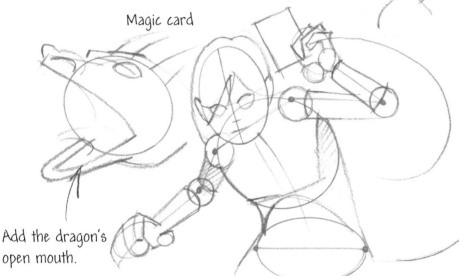

Add the dragon's open mouth.

3. Draw stick arms and legs with dots for the joints and outline shapes for the hands.

4. Using your construction lines as a guide, draw the main shapes of the body and the position of the facial features.

5. Add detail to the face, hair, and costume of dragon girl. Build up the features of the dragon as you go along.

Add movement lines to this dramatic pose.

24

6. Erase the construction lines if you want to, then finish off all remaining details and add shading.

Practice drawing hands gripping objects.

Take time with the details of the dragon's head. Sharp teeth, nostrils, and horns all help to add to its monstrous appearance.

Add shade to areas light wouldn't reach.

The pose of dragon girl creates folds and creases in her clothes. Think about how to shade these areas.

Instead of shading your drawing you can try finishing your drawing in ink. Go over all outlines in ink and remove any pencil lines.

ninja

Moving silently through the night, the ninja is the master of stealth, spying on people unnoticed.

1. Draw circles for the head and body and an oval for the hips. Sketch lines for the spine and the angles of the hips and shoulders, with dots to position the joints.

2. Draw stick arms and legs, with basic shapes for the hands and feet.

This is a strong hero pose. Look at pictures of martial arts masters to get an idea of how the legs should bend.

3. Now start to outline the arms, legs, and torso. Add some facial features. Remember, eyes and ears are always on the center line!

Draw circles for knees and elbows.

Don't forget to use your construction lines as a guide when drawing the basic shapes of the body.

26

4. Now sketch in the basic shapes of the clothes and mask. Think about how the robes will crease at the knees, chest, and groin.

We cannot see the other arm, but use construction lines to ensure the hand is proportioned correctly.

Three fingers up

Trousers are tied just below the knee.

5. Erase your construction lines and take your time to finish all the details, like the folds and shading in the clothes.

Belt detail

The ninja looks great finished off in ink. Try drawing her in silhouette, too!

monkey

onkey is young, brash, and very brave. He is rebellious and will break any rules to help fight crime and save people. He can swing from rooftop to rooftop.

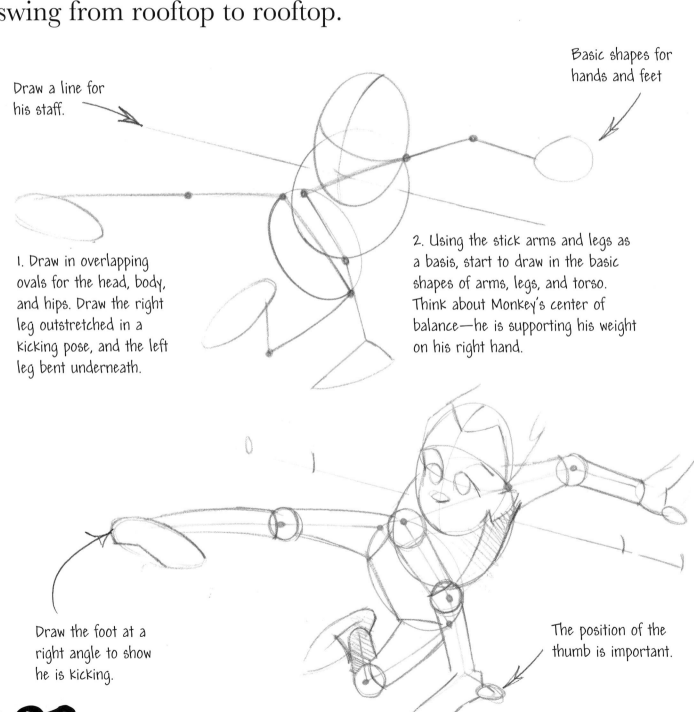

Draw a line for his staff.

Basic shapes for hands and feet

1. Draw in overlapping ovals for the head, body, and hips. Draw the right leg outstretched in a kicking pose, and the left leg bent underneath.

2. Using the stick arms and legs as a basis, start to draw in the basic shapes of arms, legs, and torso. Think about Monkey's center of balance—he is supporting his weight on his right hand.

Draw the foot at a right angle to show he is kicking.

The position of the thumb is important.

3. Start drawing the details, such as the clothes, hair, and facial features.

Drawing the hair like this gives the impression he is moving very fast!

Monkey tail

This is a good picture to practice drawing creases and folds. There are lots of creases because Monkey is moving fast.

4. Erase construction lines before adding final details.

Try adding little details like the headgear.

Larger eyes with highlights let us know Monkey is a child. (see p. 15)

Highlights in the hair.

Here's the same drawing finished in ink. Remove any leftover pencil lines.

29

robo-captain

The robo-captain is half man, half machine, and he comes from the future. He is invincible, he can fly, and he protects everyone from danger. Everyone's safe when the captain's around!

1. Draw the ovals and construction lines for a basic standing pose. Remember, draw stick arms and legs with dots for joints.

We won't see the facial features in the finished picture, but it is still important to position them.

Basic shapes for hands and feet

2. Sketch the arms and legs. This is a good, solid hero pose. Drawing the fists clenched will add drama to the figure.

Add circles for knees, elbows, and shoulders.

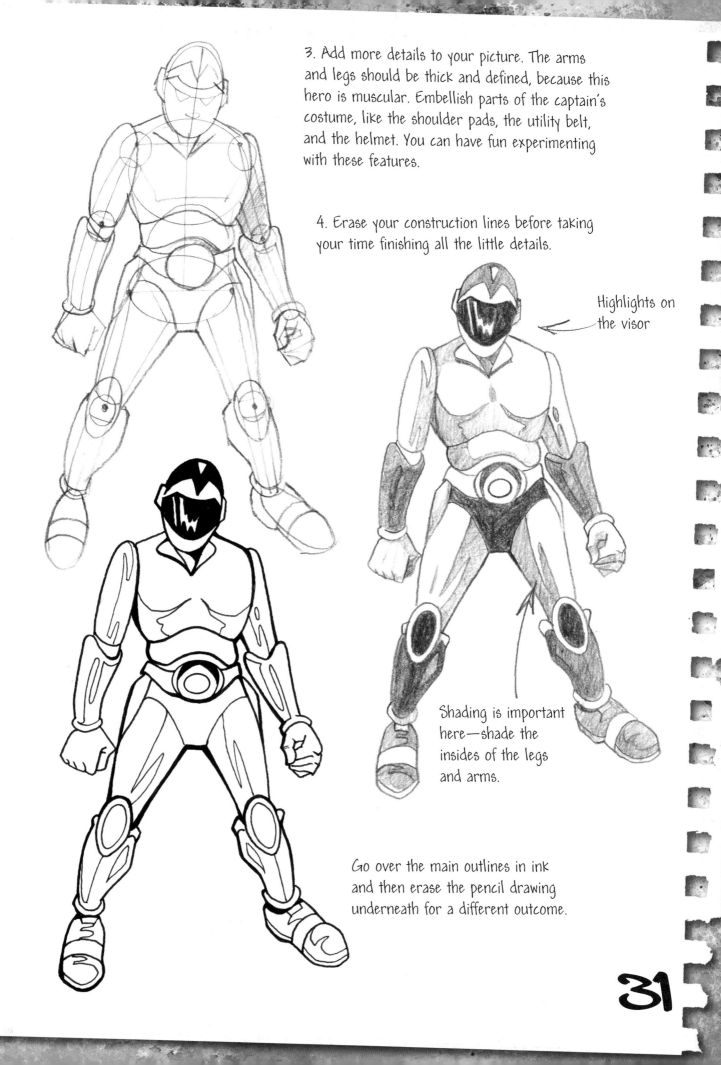

3. Add more details to your picture. The arms and legs should be thick and defined, because this hero is muscular. Embellish parts of the captain's costume, like the shoulder pads, the utility belt, and the helmet. You can have fun experimenting with these features.

4. Erase your construction lines before taking your time finishing all the little details.

Highlights on the visor

Shading is important here—shade the insides of the legs and arms.

Go over the main outlines in ink and then erase the pencil drawing underneath for a different outcome.

31

glossary

Composition The positioning of the various parts of a picture on the drawing paper.

Construction lines Guidelines used in the early stages of a drawing which are usually erased later.

Cross-hatching A series of criss-crossing lines used to add shade to a drawing.

Hatching A series of parallel lines used to add shade to a drawing.

Manga A Japanese word for "comic" or "cartoon"; also the style of drawing that is used in Japanese comics.

Silhouette A drawing that shows only a dark shape, like a shadow, sometimes with a few details left white.

Three-dimensional Having an effect of depth, so as to look like a real character rather than a flat picture.

Tone The contrast between light and shade that helps to add depth to a picture.

Vanishing point The place in a perspective drawing where parallel lines appear to meet.

index